NIGHT PRAYER

1976
Publications Office
UNITED STATES CATHOLIC CONFERENCE
1312 Massachusetts Avenue, N.W.
Washington, D.C. 20005

Psalm Commentaries

The commentaries, presented in this booklet, have been prepared by Rev. Stephen Hartdegen, O.F.M., Coordinator for Program Development, U.S. Catholic Conference and Director of the U.S. Center for the Catholic Biblical Apostolate.

CONTENTS

ACKNOWLEDGMENTS

The International Committee on English in the Liturgy, Inc., is grateful to the following for permission to reproduce copyright material:

Hymns

Benedictine Nuns of Saint Mary's Abbey, West Malling, Sussex, for "We praise you, Father, for your gift."

Geoffrey Chapman Publishers, for James Quinn, S.J., "Day is done but love unfailing," "Now at the daylight's ending."

Fides Publishers, Inc., Notre Dame, Indiana, for "All praise to you, O God, this night," and "O radiant Light, O Sun divine," from *Morning Praise and Evensong* © 1973 copyright by Fides Publishers, Inc.

Jerome Leamon, for "Lord Jesus Christ, abide with us."

World Library Publications, Inc., 2145 Central Parkway, Cincinnati, Ohio, for Rev. M. Quinn, O.P., "O Christ you are the light and day," © copyright 1965 by World Library Publications.

Religious Poetry

William Heinemann Ltd., London, for Arthur Symons, "Lines Written in Her Breviary: Let Nothing Disturb Thee," and "If, Lord, Thy Love for Me Is Strong," from the *Poems of Arthur Symons.*

Oxford University Press, London, for "O Deus Ego Amo Te" from *Poems of Gerard Manley Hopkins* (4th edition) edited by W. H. Gardner and N. H. Mackenzie, published by Oxford University Press by arrangement with the Society of Jesus, and for "Thou Art Indeed Just, Lord" by Gerard Manley Hopkins from the *Oxford Book of English Mystical Verse,* published by Oxford University Press.

Psalms

Permission has been granted by the Grail (England) for inclusion of psalms from: *The Psalms: A New Translation* © the Grail (England) 1963.

The complete Psalms first published in 1963 by and available through Wm. Collins Sons & Co., Limited. In North America through the Paulist Press Inc. and Collins and World.

Art and Layout: Ems Bolle

INTRODUCTION

Night prayer still remains a part of the rhythm of daily prayer among many Catholics. Whereas it has frequently taken on a very personal character, composed of one's own select prayers, in other cases it has become the common prayer of a particular group, as for example the family, at the end of the day.

This booklet offers individuals and groups the opportunity to use Night Prayer as presented in the Liturgy of the Hours restored by the Second Vatican Council. As an excerpt from the Divine Office it offers all of the faithful the possibility of participating in the prayer of the Church, praying in union with Christ to the Father.

INTRODUCTION

Night Prayer as found in the Liturgy of the Hours is the last prayer of one's day, said just before going to bed, even if it is past midnight. It may be prayed with others—a practice which is highly encouraged—or alone. The father or mother of the family could, for example, lead the family in this common night prayer from the Office.

STRUCTURE

Introduction

Like the other hours of the Liturgy of the Hours, Night Prayer begins with the introductory verse *God, come to my assistance,* and the *Glory to the Father* to which the *Alleluia* is added outside of Lent. Basically, the introduction is a call to prayer and a brief expression of praise.

Examination of Conscience

Immediately after the introduction there is an examination of conscience—a review of the day in the presence of God. In communal celebrations a penitential rite, as at Mass, may be used (See Appendix I). When prayed alone, a brief pause for reflection might be followed by a short penitential prayer (See Appendix I).

Hymn

An appropriate hymn follows to set the tone of Night Prayer. Hymns are provided in place within this booklet; others may be substituted, but care should be taken that they fit into the context of Night Prayer.

When prayed in common, the hymn is sung. In private it could be recited or replaced by an appropriate poem (See Appendix III).

Psalmody

The psalms are the heart of the Liturgy of the Hours and have been carefully chosen to correspond to the hour of the day. In Night Prayer psalms have been selected which evoke confidence in God. Although each day has a selected psalm or psalms, one may always substitute the Saturday or Sunday psalms on weekdays; this might be helpful for those who would like to pray Night Prayer from memory.

The psalm is concluded with the *Glory to the Father* giving the prayer of the Old Testament a quality of praise as well as adding a christological and trinitarian dimension.

An antiphon is provided for each psalm and serves to briefly state the theme of the psalm, illustrate the literary character of the psalm, and to turn the psalm into a personal prayer, highlighting a certain significant phrase which might easily be missed. On occasion (especially when prayed by a group) the antiphon may be used as a response after each verse of the psalm, in the manner of the responsorial psalm of the liturgy of the word in the eucharist.

Psalm-prayer

A psalm-prayer has been provided for the end of each psalm. After the psalm has been prayed, the antiphon repeated, and a brief period of silence observed, the prayer is said. It sums up the thoughts and feelings of those who just prayed and helps one to see the psalm in a Christian light.

Reading and Response

A short reading from scripture follows the psalm-prayer and should be read and received as a true proclamation of God's word. The passages chosen for Night Prayer are appropriate for the time of day as they refer to images such as night, sleep, rest, etc.

The response to the reading may be twofold: silent reflection and the responsory *Into your hands, . . .* **As a type of acclamation the response enables God's word to penetrate more deeply into the minds and hearts of those who are praying.**

Gospel Canticle

The Canticle of Simeon (Luke 2:29-32) is said at Night Prayer throughout the week. The canticle expresses the faith and confidence of Simeon in God's wonderful work of salvation: Jesus Christ.

Prayer

A concluding prayer, which varies with each night, follows immediately. It attempts to sum up the entire intention of Night Prayer in the form of a final petition addressed to God the Father.

Conclusion: Blessing, Marian Antiphon

After the final prayer, the blessing *May the all-powerful Lord* is said, even when Night Prayer is said alone.

Finally, one of the antiphons in honor of the Blessed Virgin is said (See Appendix II).

SUNDAY

INTRODUCTION

God, come to my assistance.
—Lord, make haste to help me.

Glory to the Father, and to the Son, and to the
　　　Holy Spirit:

as it was in the beginning, is now, and will be for
　　　ever. Amen.

*A brief examination of conscience may be made. At its con-
clusion one of the penitential prayers in Appendix I may be
said.*

HYMN

O Christ, you are the light and day
Which drives away the night,
The ever shining Sun of God
And pledge of future light.

As now the ev'ning shadows fall
Please grant us, Lord, we pray,
A quiet night to rest in you
Until the break of day.

Remember us, poor mortal men,
We humbly ask, O Lord,
And may your presence in our souls
Be now our great reward.

Melody: Saint Anne C.M.   *Music: William Croft, 1708*
Text: Christe qui Lux es et Dies
Translator: Rev. M. Quinn, O.P., et al.

PSALMODY

Ant.   **Night holds no terrors for me sleeping under God's wings.**

Psalm 91

Safe in God's sheltering care

I have given you the power to tread upon serpents and scorpions (Luke 10:19).

He who dwells in the shelter of
    the Most High
and abides in the shade of the Almighty
says to the Lord: "My refuge,
my stronghold, my God in whom I trust!"

It is he who will free you from the snare
of the fowler who seeks to destroy you;
he will conceal you with his pinions
and under his wings you will find refuge.

You will not fear the terror of the night
nor the arrow that flies by day,
nor the plague that prowls in the darkness
nor the scourge that lays waste at noon.

A thousand may fall at your side,
ten thousand fall at your right,
you, it will never approach;
his faithfulness is buckler and shield.

Your eyes have only to look
to see how the wicked are repaid,
you who have said: "Lord, my refuge!"
and have made the Most High your dwelling.

3

Upon you no evil shall fall,
no plague approach where you dwell.
For you has he commanded his angels,
to keep you in all your ways.

They shall bear you upon their hands
lest you strike your foot against a stone.
On the lion and the viper you will tread
and trample the young lion and the dragon.

Since he clings to me in love, I will free him;
protect him for he knows my name.
When he calls I shall answer: "I am with
     you."
I will save him in distress and give him glory.

With length of life I will content him;
I shall let him see my saving power.

PSALM-PRAYER

Lord Jesus Christ, when tempted by the devil,
you remained loyal to your Father whose angels
watched over you at his command. Guard your
Church and keep us safe from the plague of sin
so that we may remain loyal to the day we enjoy
your salvation and your glory.

READING

Revelation 22:4-5

They shall see the Lord face to face and bear his name on their foreheads. The night shall be no more. They will need no light from lamps or the sun, for the Lord God shall give them light, and they shall reign forever.

RESPONSORY

Into your hands, Lord, I commend my spirit.
—Into your hands, Lord, I commend my spirit.

You have redeemed us, Lord God of truth.
—I commend my spirit.

Glory to the Father, and to the Son, and to the
    Holy Spirit.

—Into your hands, Lord, I commend my spirit.

GOSPEL CANTICLE

Luke 2:29-32

Christ is the light of the nations and the glory of Israel

Ant.   Protect us, Lord, as we stay awake; watch over us as we sleep, that awake, we may keep watch with Christ, and asleep, rest in his peace.

Lord, now you let your servant go in peace;
your word has been fulfilled:

my own eyes have seen the salvation
which you have prepared in the sight of
    every people:

a light to reveal you to the nations
and the glory of your people Israel.

PRAYER

Lord,
we have celebrated today
the mystery of the rising of Christ to new life.
May we now rest in your peace,
safe from all that could harm us,
and rise again refreshed and joyful,
to praise you throughout another day.

We ask this through Christ our Lord.

Or: on solemnities that do not occur on Sunday:
Lord,
we beg you to visit this house
and banish from it
all the deadly power of the enemy.
May your holy angels dwell here
to keep us in peace,

and may your blessing be upon us always.
We ask this through Christ our Lord.

CONCLUSION

May the all-powerful Lord grant us a restful night
and a peaceful death.
—Amen.

Antiphon of the Blessed Virgin Mary (See Appendix II).

MONDAY

INTRODUCTION

God, come to my assistance.
—Lord, make haste to help me.

Glory to the Father, and to the Son, and to the
      Holy Spirit:

as it was in the beginning, is now, and will be for
      ever. Amen.

*A brief examination of conscience may be made. At its con-
clusion one of the penitential prayers in Appendix I may be
said.*

HYMN

Day is done, but love unfailing
   Dwells ever here;
Shadows fall, but hope, prevailing,
   Calms every fear.

Loving Father, none forsaking,
Take our hearts, of Love's own making,
Watch our sleeping, guard our waking,
   Be always near.

Dark descends, but Light unending
   Shines through our night;
You are with us, ever lending
   New strength to sight;

One in love, your truth confessing,
One in hope of heaven's blessing,
May we see, in love's possessing,
   Love's endless light!

Eyes will close, but you, unsleeping,
   Watch by our side;

Death may come: in Love's safe keeping
   Still we abide.

God of love, all evil quelling,
Sin forgiving, fear dispelling,
Stay with us, our hearts indwelling,
   This eventide.

Melody: Ar Hyd Y Nos *Music:* Welsh Traditional Melody
84.84.88.84   *Text: James Quinn, S.J., 1968*

PSALMODY

Ant. **O Lord, our God, unwearied is your love for us.**

Psalm 86

Poor man's prayer in trouble

Blessed be God who comforts us in all our trials (2 Corinthians 1:3, 4).

**Turn your ear, O Lord, and give answer
for I am poor and needy.
Preserve my life, for I am faithful:
save the servant who trusts in you.**

**You are my God; have mercy on me, Lord,
for I cry to you all day long.
Give joy to your servant, O Lord,
for to you I lift up my soul.**

**O Lord, you are good and forgiving,
full of love to all who call.
Give heed, O Lord, to my prayer
and attend to the sound of my voice.**

**In the day of distress I will call
and surely you will reply.**

11

MONDAY

Among the gods there is none like you,
　　O Lord;
nor work to compare with yours.

All the nations shall come to adore you
and glorify your name, O Lord:
for you are great and do marvellous deeds,
you who alone are God.

Show me, Lord, your way
so that I may walk in your truth.
Guide my heart to fear your name.

I will praise you, Lord my God, with all my
　　heart
and glorify your name for ever;
for your love to me has been great:
you have saved me from the depths of the
　　grave.

The proud have risen against me;
ruthless men seek my life:
to you they pay no heed.

But you, God of mercy and compassion,
slow to anger, O Lord,
abounding in love and truth,
turn and take pity on me.

O give your strength to your servant
and save your handmaid's son.
Show me a sign of your favor
that my foes may see to their shame
that you console me and give me your help.

PSALM-PRAYER

God of mercy and goodness, when Christ called
out to you in torment, you heard him and gave
him victory over death because of his love for
you. We already know the affection you have
for us; fill us with a greater love of your name
and we will proclaim you more boldly before
men and happily lead them to celebrate your
glory.

READING   *1 Thessalonians 5:9-10*

God has destined us for acquiring salvation
through our Lord Jesus Christ. He died for us,
that all of us, whether awake or asleep, together
might live with him.

RESPONSORY

Into your hands, Lord, I commend my spirit.
—Into your hands, Lord, I commend my spirit.

You have redeemed us, Lord God of truth.
—I commend my spirit.

Glory to the Father, and to the Son, and to the
    Holy Spirit.

—Into your hands, Lord, I commend my spirit.

GOSPEL CANTICLE

Luke 2:29-32

Christ is the light of the nations and the glory of Israel

Ant.   **Protect us, Lord, as we stay awake;
watch over us as we sleep, that awake,
we may keep watch with Christ, and
asleep, rest in his peace.**

Lord, now you let your servant go in peace;
your word has been fulfilled:

my own eyes have seen the salvation
which you have prepared in the sight of
    every people:

a light to reveal you to the nations
and the glory of your people Israel.

14

PRAYER

> Lord,
> give our bodies restful sleep
> and let the work we have done today
> bear fruit in eternal life.
>
> We ask this through Christ our Lord.

CONCLUSION

May the all-powerful Lord grant us a restful night
and a peaceful death.
—Amen.

Antiphon of the Blessed Virgin Mary (See Appendix II).

TUESDAY

INTRODUCTION

God, come to my assistance.
—Lord, make haste to help me.

Glory to the Father, and to the Son, and to the
  Holy Spirit:

as it was in the beginning, is now, and will be for
  ever. Amen.

*A brief examination of conscience may be made. At its con-
clusion one of the penitential prayers in Appendix I may be
said.*

TUESDAY

HYMN

O radiant Light, O sun divine
Of God the Father's deathless face,
O image of the light sublime
That fills the heav'nly dwelling place.

Lord Jesus Christ, as daylight fades,
As shine the lights of eventide,
We praise the Father with the Son,
The Spirit blest and with them one.

O Son of God, the source of life,
Praise is your due by night and day;
Unsullied lips must raise the strain
Of your proclaimed and splendid name.

Melody: Jesu, dulcis memoria,
Plain Song, L.M.   *Music: Traditional*
Gregorian Melody
Text: Phos Hilaron, *Greek 3rd cent.*
Translator: William G. Storey, 1973.

PSALMODY

Ant.   **Do not hide your face from me; in you
I put my trust.**

Psalm 143: 1-11

Prayer in distress

Only by faith in Jesus Christ is a man made holy in God's sight. No observance of the law can achieve this (Galatians 2:16).

Lord, listen to my prayer:
turn your ear to my appeal.
You are faithful, you are just; give answer.
Do not call your servant to judgment
for no one is just in your sight.

The enemy pursues my soul;
he has crushed my life to the ground;
he has made me dwell in darkness
like the dead, long forgotten.
Therefore my spirit fails;
my heart is numb within me.

I remember the days that are past:
I ponder all your works.
I muse on what your hand has wrought
and to you I stretch out my hands.
Like a parched land my soul thirsts for you.

Lord, make haste and answer;
for my spirit fails within me.
Do not hide your face
lest I become like those in the grave.

In the morning let me know your love
for I put my trust in you.
Make me know the way I should walk:
to you I lift up my soul.

Rescue me, Lord, from my enemies;
I have fled to you for refuge.
Teach me to do your will
for you, O Lord, are my God.

Let your good spirit guide me
in ways that are level and smooth.
For your name's sake, Lord, save my life;
in your justice save my soul from distress.

PSALM-PRAYER

Lord Jesus, early in the morning of your resurrection, you made your love known and brought the first light of dawn to those who dwell in darkness. Your death has opened a path for us. Do not enter into judgment with your servants; let your good Spirit guide us together into the land of justice.

READING   *1 Peter 5:8-9a*

Stay sober and alert. Your opponent the devil is prowling like a roaring lion looking for someone to devour. Resist him, solid in your faith.

RESPONSORY

Into your hands, Lord, I commend my spirit.
—Into your hands, Lord, I commend my spirit.

You have redeemed us, Lord God of truth.
—I commend my spirit.

Glory to the Father, and to the Son, and to the
      Holy Spirit.

—Into your hands, Lord, I commend my spirit.

GOSPEL CANTICLE   *Luke 2:29-32*

Christ is the light of the nations and the glory of Israel

Ant.   Protect us, Lord, as we stay awake;
watch over us as we sleep, that awake,
we may keep watch with Christ, and
asleep, rest in his peace.

Lord, now you let your servant go in peace;
your word has been fulfilled:

my own eyes have seen the salvation
which you have prepared in the sight of
    every people:

a light to reveal you to the nations
and the glory of your people Israel.

21

TUESDAY

PRAYER

Lord,
fill this night with your radiance.
May we sleep in peace and rise with joy
to welcome the light of a new day in your
 name.

We ask this through Christ our Lord.

CONCLUSION

May the all-powerful Lord grant us a restful night
and a peaceful death.
—Amen.

Antiphon of the Blessed Virgin Mary (See Appendix II).

WEDNESDAY

INTRODUCTION

God, come to my assistance.
—Lord, make haste to help me.

Glory to the Father, and to the Son, and to the
    Holy Spirit:

as it was in the beginning, is now, and will be for
    ever. Amen.

*A brief examination of conscience may be made. At its con-
clusion one of the penitential prayers in Appendix I may be
said.*

WEDNESDAY

HYMN

All praise to you, O God, this night
For all the blessings of the light;
Keep us, we pray, O King of kings,
Beneath your own almighty wings.

Forgive us, Lord, through Christ your Son,
Whatever wrong this day we've done;
Your peace give to the world, O Lord,
That man might live in one accord.

Enlighten us, O blessed Light,
And give us rest throughout this night.
O strengthen us, that for your sake,
We all may serve you when we wake.

Melody: Illsley L.M.

Music: J. Bishop, 1665-1737
Text: Thomas Ken, 1709, alt.

PSALMODY

Ant.   Lord God, be my refuge and my
strength.

24

Psalm 31:1-6

Trustful prayer in adversity

Father, into your hands I commend my spirit (Luke 23:46).

In you, O Lord, I take refuge.
Let me never be put to shame.
In your justice, set me free,
hear me and speedily rescue me.

Be a rock of refuge for me,
a mighty stronghold to save me,
for you are my rock, my stronghold.
For your name's sake, lead me and guide me.

Release me from the snares they have hidden
for you are my refuge, Lord.
Into your hands I commend my spirit.
It is you who will redeem me, Lord.

PSALM-PRAYER

Full of trust we run to you, Lord, and put our
lives into your hands. You are our strength in
times of trouble and our refuge along the way.
May you be our joy at the turning points of life
and our reward at its end.

WEDNESDAY

Ant.   **Out of the depths I cry to you, Lord.**

Psalm 130

A cry from the depths

He will save his people from their sins (Matthew 1:21).

Out of the depths I cry to you, O Lord,
Lord, hear my voice!
O let your ears be attentive
to the voice of my pleading.

If you, O Lord, should mark our guilt,
Lord, who would survive?
But with you is found forgiveness:
for this we revere you.

My soul is waiting for the Lord,
I count on his word.
My soul is longing for the Lord
more than watchman for daybreak.
Let the watchman count on daybreak
and Israel on the Lord.

Because with the Lord there is mercy
and fullness of redemption,
Israel indeed he will redeem
from all its iniquity.

PSALM-PRAYER

God of might and compassion, you sent your Word into the world, a watchman to announce to men the dawn of salvation. Do not leave us in the depths of our sins but listen to your Church pleading with you. Respond to her trust, and pour out in her the fullness of your redeeming grace.

READING
Ephesians 4:26-27

If you are angry, let it be without sin. The sun must not go down on your wrath; do not give the devil a chance to work on you.

RESPONSORY

Into your hands, Lord, I commend my spirit.
—Into your hands, Lord, I commend my spirit.

You have redeemed us, Lord God of truth.
—I commend my spirit.

Glory to the Father, and to the Son, and to the
     Holy Spirit.

—Into your hands, Lord, I commend my spirit.

GOSPEL CANTICLE   *Luke 2:29-32*

Christ is the light of the nations and the glory of Israel

Ant.   **Protect us, Lord, as we stay awake;
watch over us as we sleep, that awake,
we may keep watch with Christ, and
asleep, rest in his peace.**

Lord, now you let your servant go in peace;
your word has been fulfilled:

my own eyes have seen the salvation
which you have prepared in the sight of
     every people:

a light to reveal you to the nations
and the glory of your people Israel.

PRAYER

Lord Jesus Christ,
you have given your followers
an example of gentleness and humility,
a task that is easy, a burden that is light.
Accept the prayers and work of this day,
and give us the rest that will strengthen us
to render more faithful service to you
who live and reign for ever and ever.

28

CONCLUSION

May the all-powerful Lord grant us a restful night and a peaceful death.
—Amen.

Antiphon of the Blessed Virgin Mary (See Appendix II).

THURSDAY

INTRODUCTION

God, come to my assistance.
—Lord, make haste to help me.

Glory to the Father, and to the Son, and to the
Holy Spirit:

as it was in the beginning, is now, and will be for
ever. Amen.

*A brief examination of conscience may be made. At its con-
clusion one of the penitential prayers in Appendix I may be
said.*

HYMN

Now at the daylight's ending
We turn, O God, to you:
Send forth your Holy Spirit,
Our spirit now renew.

To you in adoration,
In thankfulness and praise,
In faith and hope and gladness,
Our loving hearts we raise.

With watchful eyes, O Shepherd,
Look down upon your sheep;
Stretch forth your hands in healing
And close our eyes in sleep.

Come down, O Holy Spirit,
To be our loving Guest;
Be near us, holy angels,
And guard us as we rest.

We praise you, heav'nly Father:
From you all light descends;
You give us heaven's glory
When life's brief daylight ends.

We praise you, Jesus, Savior,
The light of heav'n above;
We praise you, Holy Spirit,
The living flame of love.

Melody: Christus Der Ist　*Music: Melchior Vulpius, 1609*
Mein Leben　　　　　　　*Text: James Quinn, S.J.*

PSALMODY

Ant.　　**In you, my God, my body will rest in hope.**

Psalm 16

God is my portion, my inheritance

The Father raised up Jesus from the dead and broke the bonds of death (Acts 2:24).

Preserve me, God, I take refuge in you.
I say to the Lord: "You are my God.
My happiness lies in you alone."

He has put into my heart a marvellous love
for the faithful ones who dwell in his land.

Those who choose other gods increase their sorrows.
Never will I offer their offerings of blood.
Never will I take their name upon my lips.

O Lord, it is you who are my portion and cup;
it is you yourself who are my prize.
The lot marked out for me is my delight:
welcome indeed the heritage that falls to me!

33

THURSDAY

I will bless the Lord who gives me counsel,
who even at night directs my heart.
I keep the Lord ever in my sight:
since he is at my right hand, I shall stand
    firm.

And so my heart rejoices, my soul is glad;
even my body shall rest in safety.
For you will not leave my soul among the
    dead,
nor let your beloved know decay.

You will show me the path of life,
the fullness of joy in your presence,
at your right hand happiness for ever.

PSALM-PRAYER

Lord Jesus, uphold those who hope in you and
give us your counsel, so that we may know the joy
of your resurrection and deserve to be among the
saints at your right hand.

READING   *1 Thessalonians 5:23*

May the God of peace make you perfect in
holiness. May he preserve you whole and entire,
spirit, soul, and body, irreproachable at the coming of our Lord Jesus Christ.

34

RESPONSORY

Into your hands, Lord, I commend my spirit.
—Into your hands, Lord, I commend my spirit.

You have redeemed us, Lord God of truth.
—I commend my spirit.

Glory to the Father, and to the Son, and to the
    Holy Spirit.

—Into your hands, Lord, I commend my spirit.

GOSPEL CANTICLE   *Luke 2:29-32*

Christ is the light of the nations and the glory of Israel

Ant.   **Protect us, Lord, as we stay awake;
watch over us as we sleep, that awake,
we may keep watch with Christ, and
asleep, rest in his peace.**

Lord, now you let your servant go in peace;
your word has been fulfilled:

my own eyes have seen the salvation
which you have prepared in the sight of
    every people:

a light to reveal you to the nations
and the glory of your people Israel.

35

THURSDAY

PRAYER

Lord God,
send peaceful sleep
to refresh our tired bodies.
May your help always renew us
and keep us strong in your service.

We ask this through Christ our Lord.

CONCLUSION

May the all-powerful Lord grant us a restful night
and a peaceful death.
—Amen.

Antiphon of the Blessed Virgin Mary (See Appendix II).

FRIDAY

INTRODUCTION

God, come to my assistance.
—Lord, make haste to help me.

Glory to the Father, and to the Son, and to the
      Holy Spirit:

as it was in the beginning, is now, and will be for
      ever. Amen.

*A brief examination of conscience may be made. At its con-
clusion one of the penitential prayers in Appendix I may be
said.*

FRIDAY

HYMN

> Lord Jesus Christ, abide with us,
> Now that the sun has run its course;
> Let hope not be obscured by night,
> But may faith's darkness be as light.
>
> Lord Jesus Christ, grant us your peace,
> And when the trials of earth shall cease,
> Grant us the morning light of grace,
> The radiant splendor of your face.
>
> Immortal, Holy, Threefold Light,
> Yours be the kingdom, pow'r, and might;
> All glory be eternally
> To you, life-giving Trinity!

Melody: Old 100th L.M.   Music: Louis Bourgeois, 1551
Text: Saint Joseph's Abbey, 1967, 1968

PSALMODY

Ant.   **Day and night I cry to you, my God.**

Psalm 88

Prayer of a sick person

This is your hour when darkness reigns (Luke 22:53).

> Lord my God, I call for help by day;
> I cry at night before you.

Let my prayer come into your presence.
O turn your ear to my cry.

For my soul is filled with evils;
my life is on the brink of the grave.
I am reckoned as one in the tomb:
I have reached the end of my strength,

like one alone among the dead;
like the slain lying in their graves;
like those you remember no more,
cut off, as they are, from your hand.

You have laid me in the depths of the tomb,
in places that are dark, in the depths.
Your anger weighs down upon me:
I am drowned beneath your waves.

You have taken away my friends
and made me hateful in their sight.
Imprisoned, I cannot escape;
my eyes are sunken with grief.

I call to you, Lord, all the day long;
to you I stretch out my hands.
Will you work your wonders for the dead?
Will the shades stand and praise you?

Will your love be told in the grave
or your faithfulness among the dead?

Will your wonders be known in the dark
or your justice in the land of oblivion?

As for me, Lord, I call to you for help:
in the morning my prayer comes before you.
Lord, why do you reject me?
Why do you hide your face?

Wretched, close to death from my youth,
I have borne your trials; I am numb.
Your fury has swept down upon me;
your terrors have utterly destroyed me.

They surround me all the day like a flood,
they assail me all together.
Friend and neighbor you have taken away:
my one companion is darkness.

PSALM-PRAYER

Lord Jesus Christ, you chose to suffer and be
overwhelmed by death in order to open the gates
of death in triumph. Stay with us to help us on
our pilgrimage; free us from all evil by the power
of your resurrection. In the company of your
saints, and constantly remembering your love for
us, may we sing of your wonders in our Father's
house.

READING

Jeremiah 14:9a

You are in our midst, O Lord,
> your name we bear:
> do not forsake us, O Lord, our God!

RESPONSORY

Into your hands, Lord, I commend my spirit.
—Into your hands, Lord, I commend my spirit.

You have redeemed us, Lord God of truth.
—I commend my spirit.

Glory to the Father, and to the Son, and to the
> Holy Spirit.

—Into your hands, Lord, I commend my spirit.

GOSPEL CANTICLE

Luke 2:29-32

Christ is the light of the nations and the glory of Israel

Ant.   **Protect us, Lord, as we stay awake; watch over us as we sleep, that awake, we may keep watch with Christ, and asleep, rest in his peace.**

Lord, now you let your servant go in peace;
your word has been fulfilled:

my own eyes have seen the salvation
which you have prepared in the sight of
   every people:

a light to reveal you to the nations
and the glory of your people Israel.

PRAYER

All-powerful God,
keep us united with your Son
in his death and burial
so that we may rise to new life with him,
who lives and reigns for ever and ever.

CONCLUSION

May the all-powerful Lord grant us a restful night
and a peaceful death.
—Amen.

Antiphon of the Blessed Virgin Mary (See Appendix II).

SATURDAY

INTRODUCTION

God, come to my assistance.
—Lord, make haste to help me.

Glory to the Father, and to the Son, and to the
Holy Spirit:

as it was in the beginning, is now, and will be for
ever. Amen.

*A brief examination of conscience may be made. At its con-
clusion one of the penitential prayers in Appendix I may be
said.*

SATURDAY

HYMN

We praise you, Father, for your gifts
Of dusk and nightfall over earth,
Foreshadowing the mystery
Of death that leads to endless day.

Within your hands we rest secure;
In quiet sleep our strength renew;
Yet give your people hearts that wake
In love to you, unsleeping Lord.

Your glory may we ever seek
In rest, as in activity,
Until its fullness is revealed,
O source of life, O Trinity.

Melody: Te lucis ante terminum (plainchant) Music: Anon.,
L.M.   *Gregorian*
                              Text: West Malling Abbey

PSALMODY

Ant.   Have mercy, Lord, and hear my prayer.

Psalm 4

Thanksgiving

The resurrection of Christ was God's supreme and wholly marvelous work (Saint Augustine).

When I call, answer me, O God of justice;
from anguish you released me; have mercy
and hear me!

O men, how long will your hearts be closed,
will you love what is futile and seek what is
false?

It is the Lord who grants favors to those
whom he loves;
the Lord hears me whenever I call him.

Fear him; do not sin: ponder on your bed
and be still.
Make justice your sacrifice and trust in the
Lord.

"What can bring us happiness?" many say.
Let the light of your face shine on us,
O Lord.

You have put into my heart a greater joy
than they have from abundance of corn and
new wine.

I will lie down in peace and sleep comes at
   once
for you alone, Lord, make me dwell in
   safety.

PSALM-PRAYER

You consoled your Son in his anguish and released
him from the darkness of the grave. Lord, turn
your face toward us that we may sleep in your
peace and rise in your light.

Ant.   In the silent hours of night, bless the
         Lord.

Psalm 134

Evening prayer in the Temple

*Praise our God, all you his servants, you who fear him,
small and great* (Revelation 19:5).

O come, bless the Lord,
all you who serve the Lord,
who stand in the house of the Lord,
in the courts of the house of our God.

Lift up your hands to the holy place
and bless the Lord through the night.

May the Lord bless you from Zion,
he who made both heaven and earth.

PSALM-PRAYER

All your servants praise and thank you, Lord. Be our light as night descends. We lift up to you the good works of our hands; grant us your generous blessing.

READING   *Deuteronomy 6:4-7*

Hear, O Israel! The Lord is our God, the Lord alone! Therefore, you shall love the Lord, your God, with all your heart, and with all your soul, and with all your strength. Take to heart these words which I enjoin on you today. Drill them into your children. Speak of them at home and abroad, whether you are busy or at rest.

RESPONSORY

Into your hands, Lord, I commend my spirit.
—Into your hands, Lord, I commend my spirit.

SATURDAY

You have redeemed us, Lord God of truth.
—I commend my spirit.

Glory to the Father, and to the Son, and to the
Holy Spirit.

—Into your hands, Lord, I commend my spirit.

GOSPEL CANTICLE   *Luke 2:29-32*

Christ is the light of the nations and the glory of Israel

Ant.   **Protect us, Lord, as we stay awake;
watch over us as we sleep, that awake,
we may keep watch with Christ, and
asleep, rest in his peace.**

Lord, now you let your servant go in peace;
your word has been fulfilled:

my own eyes have seen the salvation
which you have prepared in the sight of
every people:

a light to reveal you to the nations
and the glory of your people Israel.

PRAYER

Lord,
be with us throughout this night.
When day comes may we rise from sleep
to rejoice in the resurrection of your Christ,
who lives and reigns for ever and ever.

Or:

Lord,
we beg you to visit this house
and banish from it
all the deadly power of the enemy.
May your holy angels dwell here
to keep us in peace,
and may your blessing be upon us always.

We ask this through Christ our Lord.

CONCLUSION

May the all-powerful Lord grant us a restful night
and a peaceful death.
—Amen.

Antiphon of the Blessed Virgin Mary (See Appendix II).

APPENDIX I
PRAYERS FOR FORGIVENESS

When Night Prayer is prayed alone, a brief pause for reflection might be followed by one of the following short penitential prayers:

1.

**I confess to almighty God,
and to you, my brothers and sisters,
that I have sinned through my own fault
in my thoughts and in my words,
in what I have done,
and in what I have failed to do;
and I ask blessed Mary, ever virgin,
all the angels and saints,
and you, my brothers and sisters,
to pray for me to the Lord our God.**

2.

My God,
I am sorry for my sins with all my heart.
In choosing to do wrong
and failing to do good,
I have sinned against you
whom I should love above all things.
I firmly intend, with your help,
to do penance,
to sin no more,
and to avoid whatever leads me to sin.
Our Savior Jesus Christ
suffered and died for us.
In his name, my God, have mercy.

3.

Remember, Lord, your compassion and mercy
which you showed long ago.
Do not recall the sins and failings of my youth.
In your mercy remember me, Lord, because of
      your goodness.

Psalm 25:6-7

4.

Wash me from my guilt
and cleanse me of my sin.
I acknowledge my offense;
my sin is before me always.

Psalm 51:4-5

5.

Father, I have sinned against you
and am not worthy to be called your son.
Be merciful to me, a sinner.

Luke 15:18; 18:13

6.

Father of mercy,
like the prodigal son
I return to you and say:
"I have sinned against you
and am no longer worthy to be called your son."
Christ Jesus, Savior of the world,
I pray with the repentant thief
to whom you promised Paradise:
"Lord, remember me in your kingdom."
Holy Spirit, fountain of love,
I call on you with trust:
"Purify my heart,
and help me to walk as a child of light."

7.

Lord Jesus,
you opened the eyes of the blind,
healed the sick,
forgave the sinful woman,
and after Peter's denial confirmed him in your
      love.

APPENDIX I

Listen to my prayer:
forgive all my sins,
renew your love in my heart,
help me to live in perfect unity with my fellow
  Christians
that I may proclaim your saving power to all the
  world.

For group celebrations the following penitential forms may be used:

54

Introduction

The celebrant invites everyone to recall their sins and to repent of them in silence. He/she may use these or similar words:

**Coming together as God's family,
with confidence let us ask the Father's forgiveness,
for he is full of gentleness and compassion.**

A.

All say:

**I confess to almighty God,
and to you, my brothers and sisters,
that I have sinned through my own fault
in my thoughts and in my words,
in what I have done,
and in what I have failed to do;
and I ask blessed Mary, ever virgin,
all the angels and saints,
and you, my brothers and sisters,
to pray for me to the Lord our God.**

The celebrant says the absolution:
**May almighty God have mercy on us,
forgive us our sins,
and bring us to everlasting life.**

All answer:
Amen.

B.

The celebrant says:

Lord, we have sinned against you:

All answer:

Lord, have mercy.

Celebrant:

Lord, show us your mercy and love.

All:

And grant us your salvation.

The celebrant says the absolution:

**May almighty God have mercy on us,
forgive us our sins,
and bring us to everlasting life.**

All answer:

Amen.

C.

*The celebrant makes the following or other
invocations:*

i

Celebrant:
You were sent to heal the contrite:
Lord, have mercy.

All answer:
Lord, have mercy.

Celebrant:
You came to call sinners:
Christ, have mercy.

All:
Christ, have mercy.

Celebrant:
You plead for us at the right hand of the Father:
Lord, have mercy.

All:
Lord, have mercy.

The celebrant says the absolution:
May almighty God have mercy on us,
forgive us our sins,
and bring us to everlasting life.

All answer:
Amen.

ii

Celebrant:
**Lord Jesus, you came to reconcile us
to one another and to the Father:
Lord, have mercy.**

All answer:
Lord, have mercy.

Celebrant:
**Lord Jesus, you heal the wounds of sin and
division:
Christ, have mercy.**

All:
Christ, have mercy.

Celebrant:
**Lord Jesus, you intercede for us with your
Father:
Lord, have mercy.**

All:
Lord, have mercy.

The celebrant says the absolution:
**May almighty God have mercy on us,
forgive us our sins,
and bring us to everlasting life.**

All answer:
Amen.

iii

Celebrant:

**You raise the dead to life in the Spirit:
Lord, have mercy.**

All answer:

Lord, have mercy.

Celebrant:

**You bring pardon and peace to the sinner:
Christ, have mercy.**

All:

Christ, have mercy.

Celebrant:

**You bring light to those in darkness:
Lord, have mercy.**

All:

Lord, have mercy.

The celebrant says the absolution:

**May almighty God have mercy on us,
forgive us our sins,
and bring us to everlasting life.**

All answer:

Amen.

APPENDIX I

iv

Celebrant:
Lord Jesus, you healed the sick:
Lord, have mercy.

All answer:
Lord, have mercy.

Celebrant:
Lord Jesus, you forgave sinners:
Christ, have mercy.

All:
Christ, have mercy.

Celebrant:
Lord Jesus, you give us yourself to heal us and
bring us strength:
Lord, have mercy.

All:
Lord, have mercy.

The celebrant says the absolution:
May almighty God have mercy on us,
forgive us our sins,
and bring us to everlasting life.

All answer:
Amen.

APPENDIX II
ANTIPHONS IN HONOR OF
THE BLESSED VIRGIN

1.

Hail, holy Queen, mother of mercy,
our life, our sweetness, and our hope.
To you do we cry,
poor banished children of Eve.
To you do we send up our sighs
mourning and weeping in this vale of tears.
Turn then, most gracious advocate,
your eyes of mercy toward us,
and after this exile
show us the blessed fruit of your womb, Jesus.
O clement, O loving,
O sweet Virgin Mary.

2.

Loving mother of the Redeemer,
gate of heaven, star of the sea,
assist your people who have fallen yet strive to
     rise again.

To the wonderment of nature you bore your
     Creator,
yet remained a virgin after as before.
You who received Gabriel's joyful greeting,
have pity on us poor sinners.

3.

Hail Mary, full of grace,
the Lord is with you!
Blessed are you among women,
and blessed is the fruit of your womb, Jesus.
Holy Mary, Mother of God,
pray for us sinners,
now and at the hour of our death.

4.

Queen of heaven, rejoice, alleluia.
The Son whom you merited to bear, alleluia,
has risen as he said, alleluia.

Rejoice and be glad, O Virgin Mary, alleluia!
For the Lord has truly risen, alleluia.

APPENDIX III
POETRY SELECTIONS

ABIDE WITH ME

Abide with me; fast falls the eventide;
The darkness deepens; Lord, with me abide;
When other helpers fail, and comforts flee,
Help of the helpless, O abide with me.

Swift to its close ebbs out life's little day;
Earth's joys grow dim, its glories pass away;
Change and decay in all around I see;
O thou who changest not, abide with me.

Hold thou thy Cross before my closing eyes;
Shine through the gloom, and point me to the
      skies;
Heaven's morning breaks, and earth's vain
      shadows flee;
In life, in death, O Lord, abide with me.

H. F. Lyte

LINES WRITTEN IN HER BREVIARY

Let nothing disturb thee,
Nothing affright thee;
All things are passing;
God never changeth;
Patient endurance
Attaineth to all things;
Who God possesseth
In nothing is wanting;
Alone God sufficeth.

Saint Teresa
Translator: Arthur Symons

A HYMN TO GOD THE FATHER

Wilt Thou forgive that sin where I begun,
　Which was my sin, though it were done before?
Wilt Thou forgive that sin through which I run,
　And do run still, though still I do deplore?
　　When Thou hast done, Thou hast not done,
　　For I have more.

Wilt Thou forgive that sin which I have won
　Others to sin? and made my sin their door?
Wilt Thou forgive that sin which I did shun
　A year or two, but wallowed in a score?
　　When Thou hast done, Thou hast not done,
　　For I have more.

I have a sin of fear, that when I have spun
　My last thread, I shall perish on the shore;
But swear by Thy self, that at my death Thy Son
　Shall shine as he shines now and heretofore;
　　And, having done that, Thou hast done,
　　I fear no more.

John Donne

O DEUS EGO AMO TE

O God, I love thee, I love thee—
Not out of hope of heaven for me
Nor fearing not to love and be
   In the everlasting burning.
Thou, thou, my Jesus, after me
   Didst reach thine arms out dying,
For my sake sufferedst nails and lance,
Mocked and marred countenance,
   Sorrows passing number,
   Sweat and care and cumber,
Yea and death, and this for me,
   And thou couldst see me sinning:
Then I, why should not I love thee,
Jesu, so much in love with me?
Not for heaven's sake; not to be
Out of hell by loving thee;
Not for any gains I see;
But just the way that thou didst me
I do love and I will love thee;
What must I love thee, Lord, for then?
For being my king and God. Amen.

Gerard Manley Hopkins

IF, LORD, THY LOVE FOR ME
IS STRONG

If, Lord, Thy love for me is strong
As this which binds me unto Thee,
What holds me from Thee, Lord, so long,
What holds Thee, Lord, so long from me?

O soul, what then desirest thou?
—Lord, I would see, who thus choose Thee.
What fears can yet assail thee now?
—All that I fear is to lose Thee.

Love's whole possession I entreat,
Lord, make my soul Thine own abode,
And I will build a nest so sweet
It may not be too poor for God.

O soul in God hidden from sin,
What more desires for thee remain,
Save but to love, and love again,
And all on flame with love within,
Love on, and turn to love again?

Saint Teresa
Translator: Arthur Symons

THOU ART INDEED JUST, LORD

Justus quidem tu es, Domine, si disputem tecum:
verumtamen justa loquar ad te: Quare via impiorum
prosperatur? Etc.: [Jeremiah xii.i]

Thou art indeed just, Lord, if I contend
With thee; but, sir, so what I plead is just.
Why do sinners' ways prosper? and why must
Disappointment all I endeavour end?
　　Wert thou my enemy, O thou my friend,
How wouldst thou worse, I wonder, than thou
　　　　dost
Defeat, thwart me? Oh, the sots and thralls of lust
Do in spare hours more thrive than I that spend,
Sir, life upon thy cause. See, banks and brakes
Now, leaved how thick! laced they are again
With fretty chervil, look, and fresh wind shakes
Them; birds build—but not I build; no, but
　　　　strain,
Time's eunuch, and not breed one work that
　　　　wakes.
Mine, O thou lord of life, send my roots rain.

Gerard Manley Hopkins

LEAD, KINDLY LIGHT

Lead, kindly Light, amid the encircling gloom,
Lead thou me on;
The night is dark, and I am far from home,
Lead thou me on.
Keep thou my feet; I do not ask to see
The distant scene; one step enough for me.

I was not ever thus, nor prayed that thou
Shouldst lead me on;
I loved to choose and see my path; but now
Lead thou me on.
I loved the garish day, and, spite of fears,
Pride ruled my will: remember not past years.

So long thy power hath blest me, sure it still
Will lead me on
O'er moor and fen, o'er crag and torrent, till
The night is gone,
And with the morn those Angel faces smile,
Which I have loved long since, and lost awhile.

J. H. Newman

APPENDIX IV
COMMENTARY ON
NIGHT PRAYER PSALMS

INTRODUCTION

The psalms have always been an important part of Christian prayer. In a sense they belong to no specific age for they speak a universal language and express the human and religious experience of all peoples.

There are nine psalms used in Night Prayer as presented in the Liturgy of the Hours and included in this booklet. The following commentaries on the night prayer psalms have been prepared to assist the reader to pray them with greater understanding and at the same time to offer material for prayerful reflection.

SUNDAY:
PSALM 91

Safe in God's sheltering care

The man who believes and trusts in God finds security against the perils of this life "in the shelter," i.e., under the protection "of the Almighty" (1). The psalmist describes these perils under the figures of snares and of destroying pestilence (3). He regards them as the work of malevolent spirits, provoking crises at each of the four periods of the day: at night, in the morning, at noonday and in the evening (5-6). These are balanced by the four harmful animals; the asp, the viper, the lion and the dragon (13). All together these figures portray in poetic fashion the innumerable threats to human safety. By contrast, however, they serve but to enhance the masterful power of God's care and protection variously designated as "shelter, fortress, refuge, wings, shield and buckler" capable of surmounting every obstacle (1, 2, 4, 9). "Upon you no evil shall fall, no plague approach where you dwell." (10)

The divine protection accorded the person who believes and trusts in God is not to be understood as freedom from every physical and material affliction, or from every adversity, but as divine assistance to convert these into greater likeness to Christ and increasing participation in his redemptive suffering, death and resurrection to glory. His own words reassure us, "Do not fear those who deprive the body of life but cannot destroy the soul." (Mt 10, 28).

Security under God's protection finds its fullest realization in Christ and through him is reflected in us. Why? Because Jesus as man, united to God, renders him supreme worship and thus triumphs over sin and Satan and death. And we, in turn, are called to "cling to," i.e., be united with him and "to acknowledge and call upon his name" which is, to worship him, in Christ and through Christ. Thus we are made worthy to receive from God the comforting assurance of his protection of the just man:

"I will be with him in distress,
I will deliver him and glorify him;
I will show him my salvation." (16)

"If God is for us, who can be against us?" (Rom 8, 31)

MONDAY: PSALM 86

Poor man's prayer in trouble

This prayer is a desperate cry for help from an afflicted man in deep distress (1, 6, 7). His trouble is both spiritual and physical. To the insults of the haughty was joined the threat of death at the hands of cruel persecutors (14). His plea is at once an acknowledgment of utter helplessness and of need for assistance as well as an expression of confidence in receiving it, based on God's universal sovereignty and power (2, 7, 8-10).

The afflicted man does not complain. He does not ask God why he lets distress happen to him. He actually praises God, thanks him sincerely (12), asks forgiveness (5), and confidently presents his plea for help (2, 3, 4, 16-17). Thus he exemplifies the four ends of divine worship. Previous experience of assistance (8-10, 13) increases his confidence in receiving it this time also, despite his present misery.

What means of help does this man seek from God to raise him up from his extreme distress? Note that they are spiritual means! "Show me, Lord, your way. . . . guide my heart. . . ." He asks to know God better, to learn more about his ways of mercy, kindness, patience and fidelity (11, 13, 15) so that he may walk in God's truth with all his heart, that is, conduct himself steadfastly with singleness of purpose, with profound reverence, devotion and worshipful love of God (11, 12).

Faced with imminent peril, this saintly man, accustomed to affliction and trust in God, needs help at once. He ends his prayer asking for pity, strength, rescue, and a sign of divine favor to restore his security and confound his persecutors (16-17).

In this man's plight we identify our own problem in relation to evil men and, in general, to all adverse circumstances of life that threaten our welfare. Our spiritual need for divine assistance is no less great than that of the psalmist.

In all this Christ is our example "who bore our infirmities and endured our sufferings" (Is 53, 4). He is also the model for us to walk the ways of God in truth with our whole heart in worshipful love of God, for he is "the way" to the Father, "the truth and the life." By laying down his life for his friends "he took away the sins of many and won pardon for their offenses" (Is 53, 12). For this reason he is also the source of saving power that equips us to solve our ever recurring problems of dealing with evil men and with all that threatens our peace.

TUESDAY: PSALM 143

Prayer in distress

This intense prayer for deliverance reflects the extreme anxiety and distress of the suppliant. He is desperately in need of help (1). Even the confidence he has in receiving help is tested as he acknowledges his sinfulness. If brought to judgment he cannot claim innocence of wrongdoing (2).

Could it be that God is punishing the misdeeds of the petitioner or using his enemy as an instrument for correcting him? This could surely be. But the excessive cruelty of the enemy seems undeserved. He pursues, crushes to the ground, and consigns the oppressed to darkness, the dwelling of the dead (3), leaving his spirit faint and his heart appalled (4). He is made utterly helpless.

But now the suppliant remembers God's past kindnesses to Israel, and meditates on "the works of his hands," his justice, his steadfast love, his loyalty to promises, the glory of his name (5, 8, 11). These re-enkindle his hope for rescue (5, 9).

As he renews his urgent appeal for help (6) he discovers within himself a more urgent need and a more lasting goal. He is in need of instruction. He must know "the way in which he should walk" (8), how to be guided by the promptings of God's spirit and to accomplish his will. With this experience he will be able to walk "on level ground" (10), i.e., to attain the higher goal of victory over sin and oppression.

You glean from this that the deepest needs of a believing man incline him to raise his helpless hands and stretch them out to God in prayer. Only then does he perceive their power to move God to merciful response. Prayer is often prompted by present fear and accompanied by insistence on prompt response. To be mature it should rather be inspired by the reassuring memory of past mercies, the appreciation of God's patience with sinful man, the consent to do God's will. These are a greater goal than immediate relief from present distress.

Man's necessity is God's opportunity. The Incarnation is his fullest response to man's needs. Christ's coming is not due to man's merit but to God's merciful love. This holy love sustains our hope, brings victory over evil, fulfills our deepest needs. "Neither death nor life. . . . can separate us from the love of God that comes to us in Christ Jesus our Lord." (Rom 8, 38f)

WEDNESDAY: PSALM 31

Trustful prayer in adversity

Only a portion (1-6) of this long psalm is used in the night prayer for Wednesday. It should be noted that a comparison of tone and expressions with those of certain other psalms (22, 35, 61, 71) gives a two-fold impression: 1) that the author is contemplating not his own but someone else's sufferings; 2) that at least indirectly that person is the Messiah.

The psalm gives utterance to feelings of deep anguish but also of unshakeable confidence in God for help and deliverance. The anguish is due to what is described figurativley as the snare of a hunter (5). Elsewhere in the psalm the snare is seen to be a reproach based very likely on false denunciation. It provokes derision, disdain, injustice, arrogance and an attempt to bring the afflicted man to oblivion (12, 13, 18, 19).

Faithful souls beset with troubles of all kinds find in this psalm words that aptly convey the outpouring of their own souls. This is so because they are the words of the Man of Sorrows who bore our infirmities and endured our sufferings (cf Is 53,4).

"Into your hands I commend my spirit" (6), is the final prayer of the dying Christ, uttered from the height of the Cross. With it he committed himself to the Father in death. His unshakeable trust is soon vindicated by the triumph of his resurrection. This gives a new and boundless vision to religion and emphasizes the difference which Christ's life has brought to the psalms. He himself has now become their light and fulfillment. The Savior's last words summing up his life must necessarily become the fixed attitude toward God of all his true disciples. For them both the Father and the Son at his right hand become their refuge, their rock, their stronghold (2,3,4).

This psalm in its entirety can serve both as a grateful recollection of the experiences of a Christian life up to the present moment and as a sound preparation of what the future holds in store. One by one the memories pass rapidly before one's mind and heart, memories of guilt and of God's pardon, of misfortune and of the blessings of prosperity, of afflictions and of deliverance. Preparation for the future clarifies the past, leads to total and unreserved commitment of self to God until death, and to the triumph of trust in the resurrection to glory.

WEDNESDAY: PSALM 130

A cry from the depths

The psalmist represents everyone who manifests a wholesome sense of sinfulness and its consequent alienation from God (1,3). He longs for merciful forgiveness and recovery of divine favor (2,4,7). The Church in her liturgy has long used this prayer to obtain for the faithful departed release from punishment for their sins.

The soul's firm trust in God for pardon and peace springs from acknowledging man's universal proneness to sin; from the genuine fear of offending him (3-4), from the conviction that God is merciful and kind, inclined to redeem the penitent as surely as dawn follows the night (6-7).

If God were to judge us now, how could we answer for our disregard of his sovereign right to loving worship and submission? How excuse our anger in deed and speech, our selfishness, our violation of the rights of neighbor as regards his person, property and reputation? Self-warning now may spare us a judgment of condemnation at death.

Sin contradicts the supreme law of love and as such involves rebellion against God. The inherent evil of deliberate sin only penetrates us deeply when we understand that it is a repudiation of divine love. When the heart is sensitive, even little deeds and words of unkindness, neglect of opportunities for good will grieve the truly penitent soul.

"If you, O Lord, should mark our guilt . . . with you is found forgiveness." We owe thanks for sin forgiven but also profound reverence for God who forgives. The burden of our sins is lifted and its place is filled with the joy of God's mercy. At the foot of the cross "justice and peace kiss," repentance and love flow together.

THURSDAY:
PSALM 16

God is my portion, my inheritance

Psalm 16 is a meditation on the blessings of security and intimate fellowship with God. From the outset it is important to recall that in the discourse attributed to St. Peter on Pentecost he understands this psalm to refer not to David but to Christ (Acts 2,24-33).

Christ is seen then in this prophetic psalm to abide always in the presence of God the supreme good and to cherish, that is, take his delight in the fellowship of "the holy ones," the saints on the earth (1-3).

In sharp contrast he sees the plight of those "who court other gods" with their abhorrent rites of blood libations, yielding nothing but abundant sorrow. Faithful to Israelite tradition he will not even mention, much less invoke their names (4).

How rich is Christ's inheritance! His allotted portion, the division of goods, his cup of destiny, his lot of good fortune cannot be taken from him because God holds them fast. This inheritance described figuratively as a lot that allows a generous share of good land in his worship of the true God and the community of those who share it with him (5-6). In the New Testament this is seen to be the Church.

Christ's praise of the Father, his life of prayer, of communication with the Father in the quiet of the night, of living in his presence and having him at his right hand foretell the security of Jesus against falling or losing his blessed lot (7-8).

St. Peter, quoting the next verses of the psalm "My heart has been glad and my tongue has rejoiced, my body will live on in hope, for you will not suffer your faithful one to undergo corruption" says they "proclaim beforehand the resurrection of the Messiah." (Acts 2,26-28,31) The fullness of fellowship with God is seen here. Christ escapes corruption, possesses "the fullness of joy" in God's presence and at his "right hand happiness forever." (9-11)

All that is here foretold of Christ becomes our inheritance as well because our call to faith in him is also to share all things with him (Eph 1,4-10;2, 19-22). The blessings of security and intimate fellowship with God in Christ rest on the power of faith, the firmness of hope, the fidelity of love in fulfilling God's will. To give God first place in all things and to live in his presence is to enjoy the harmony and security of an integrated life with him, and to have the assurance of resurrection with Christ unto glory.

FRIDAY:
PSALM 88

Prayer of a sick person

This psalm is the plea of a man plunged in suffering due in some way to God's wrath (7). He cries out night and day to the Lord God his sole refuge, despite his apparent abandonment. His soul is steeped in utter desperation, unable to endure anymore, oppressed by God's wrath, rejected, friendless, trapped, with no means of escape. He is already counted among the dying, indeed as already dead and lying unidentified in the grave, beyond God's care, and consigned to oblivion (2-9).

A second time he cries out, stretching out his hands in prayer. And now he puts his bitterness aside for a time to ask God of what use to him is death? Will he in some way work wonders for the dead? Manifest himself in the darkness to those who have perished? Penetrate the land of oblivion so that the victims might experience his wonders, understand his justice and still have hope? (10-13). The sufferer's anguish shows clearly the need of further revelation to solve the mystery of pain and suffering.

After the third outcry and prayer of the afflicted
man — "In the morning my prayer comes before
you" — his mood of entreaty vanishes on his lips as
he is again tormented with pain. "Lord, why do you
reject me?" (14-15). Even from his youth he has been
afflicted and in agony. And now in one last lament
he says that God's furies and terrors have swept over
him like water, engulfed him, cut him off, deprived
him of friends and companions, with nothing left but
darkness (16-19).

This is the saddest of the psalms. Nowhere else in
the Scriptures do the afflictions of the just man appear
so hopeless. Nevertheless the threefold cry for help
from one who believes in God and in his power to
help tells us that man's hopelessness is never without
hope with God.

There is firm foundation for this understanding of
the psalm and for hope and consolation. Are not
these sufferings those of the Suffering Servant elsewhere described, though not all in one place (Pss
22,38,39; Isaiah 53)? The Fathers of the Church have
understood them as fulfilled in the passion and death
of Christ. Such extreme, otherwise unbearable physical pain, mental anguish and abondonment even unto
death were borne by Christ in his agony and crucifix-
ion. And they merited forgiveness and salvation for
all who repent.

The suffering Christ is the key that unlocks the
mystery of human suffering and through his own pas-

sion and death gives it redeeming value. In his rising he opens to us the gateway of our own glorious resurrection. "As we have shared much in the suffering of Christ, so through Christ do we share abundantly in his consolation." (2 Cor 1,5)

SATURDAY: PSALM 4

Thanksgiving

The psalmist is accustomed to entrust himself and his affairs to God's care. In his present need he confidently appeals to God for merciful consideration: "Have mercy and hear me" (2). The relief he desires to receive in distress is figuratively described in the original language of the psalm as a release from restriction or narrow confinement into more ample space. In this instance the release implied is from the pressures of wordly men of power and rank who would impose their godless way of life and false security on him.

·Instead he resists their pressure, takes the initiative to admonish them to recognize that God supports the man who trusts him despite all adversity, and sincerely seeks to serve him (3-4). They are to tremble, i.e., to be moved with fear at God's word and avoid sin. In offering sacrifices they are not to look for delusive omens thought to augur success for their man-made ventures but to offer just, i.e., true sacrifices, motivated by a sincere desire to know the truth (5-6).

To long for better times is also vanity if the desire is merely for greater material prosperity of abundance of grain and wine (7-8). True joy and gladness of heart is reserved for the person who relies on God and on whom in return the light of God's countenance shines and his favor rests.

Joy and peace are the blessed fruits of a life of trust in God. They are the gifts of the Spirit which earthly wisdom and prosperity cannot yield. They indicate the righteousness of the cause of those who follow this way (8-9). When trust is tested through trial and suffering, joy is all the greater and peace the more secure.

SATURDAY: PSALM 134

Evening Prayer in the Temple

As the sabbath night prayer brings to a close another week of praise of God, it is fitting that from the hearts and lips of Christians the same psalm should rise as from the ancient Jewish pilgrims at the close of their festival and octave of the feast of Booths. They exhort the priests and levites, and all the various orders of ministers about to begin their night watch to praise and bless the Lord: "O come, bless the Lord, all who serve the Lord, who stand in the house of the Lord, in the courts of the house of our God" (1). "Lift up your hands to the holy place and bless the Lord through the night" (2).

It is appropriate too that the priests respond to the song of the departing pilgrims gathered for the last time i

impart

ing in

hands

bestow

Life

by the

have n

come.

Father

before

from v

Father

their p

their b

resurre

which

and bl

them "

tion, a

gloriou

darknes

the safe

DATE DUE

3/23/67

GAYLORD

PRINTED IN U.S.